Fire Fight! THE BRAVEST

Aviation Firefighters

by Nancy White

Consultant: Stephen Kilby
Airport Division Chief
Miami–Dade County Fire Rescue Department
Miami International Airport
Miami, Florida

BEARPORT
PUBLISHING

New York, New York

Credits

Cover and Title Page, © Charles Bruno/Getty Images, © Stocktrek Images, Inc./Stocktrek, and © Vitaliy Hrabar/Fotolia; 4–5, © Andrew Cohen; 5T, © Lars Lindblad/Shutterstock; 6–7, © David R. Frazier Photolibrary/Alamy; 7, © John Bazemore/Associated Press; 8, © Dvidshub/Wikipedia Creative Commons; 9T, © Tom Mihalek/Associated Press; 9B, © Rightimage/Alamy; 10, © AlamyCelebrity/Alamy; 11, © Associated Press; 12–13, © STR/Corbis; 14T, © dpa picture alliance archive/Alamy; 14–15, © Eurostyle Graphics/Alamy; 16, © Prisma/Superstock; 17T, © Peter Holt/APN; 17B, © Zuma Press, Inc./Alamy; 18, © RuggyBearLA Photography; 19, © Justin Sullivan/Getty Images; 20–21, © Eureka/Alamy; 21, © Jeff Haynes/Getty Images; 22, © AKM-GSI/Corbis; 23R, © Danita Delimont/Alamy; 23L, © Joe Tan/Reuters/Landov; 24, © REUTERS/TVE/Handout (SPAIN); 25, © REUTERS/Juan Medina (SPAIN); 26, © Howe & Howe Technologies; 27, © FirePhoto/Alamy; 28L, © ZUMA Press, Inc./Alamy; 28R, © Charles Bruno/Getty Images; 29TL, © Brian Posey/Alamy; 29TR, © redbrickstock.com/Alamy; 29BL, © Uwe Bumann/Shutterstock; 29BR, © Ace Stock Limited/Alamy.

Publisher: Kenn Goin
Editor: Jessica Rudolph
Creative Director: Spencer Brinker
Design: Emma Randall
Photo Researcher: Ruby Tuesday Books

The author would like to thank Stephen Kilby, Division Chief of Miami–Dade Fire Rescue, and his staff for their time, the invaluable information they provided, and their inspiring enthusiasm for this project. Thanks as well for the generous help and support of Lauren Stover, Director of Security for Miami International Airport.

Library of Congress Cataloging-in-Publication Data

White, Nancy, 1942–
  Aviation firefighters / by Nancy White.
      pages cm. — (Fire fight! The bravest)
  Includes bibliographical references and index.
  Audience: Age 7–12.
  ISBN-13: 978-1-62724-096-3 (library binding)
  ISBN-10: 1-62724-096-9 (library binding)
  1. Airplanes—Fires and fire prevention—Juvenile literature. 2. Airports—Fires and fire prevention—Juvenile literature.
I. Title.
  TL697.F5W46 2014
  628.9'2—dc23
                          2013041505

For more information, write to Bearport Publishing Company, Inc., 45 West 21st Street, Suite 3B, New York, New York 10010. Printed in the United States of America.

10 9 8 7 6 5 4 3 2 1

Contents

Fire on Board!. 4

One-Minute Reaction 6

Intense Fires. 8

Poisonous Smoke 10

Evacuate!. 12

Firefighting Truck 14

Special Training 16

Behind the Scenes 18

Practice, Practice, Practice 20

Many Jobs. 22

Tragedy in Spain. 24

Science for Safety 26

Aviation Firefighters' Gear 28

Glossary 30

Bibliography 31

Read More. 31

Learn More Online. 31

Index 32

About the Author. 32

Fire on Board!

Everything seemed fine on the evening of June 8, 1995, at Hartsfield-Jackson International Airport in Atlanta, Georgia. However, just as ValuJet Flight 597 was about to take off, the flight's **crew** and passengers heard a loud bang. Seconds later, flames and thick black smoke poured into the **cabin** where the passengers sat.

The pilot immediately stopped the plane on the **runway** and called the control tower. "We have a fire in the right engine!" he shouted into the radio. "Roll the equipment," he continued, which meant, "Call out the **aviation** firefighters!" Within moments, they were speeding to the scene.

A control tower at Hartsfield-Jackson Airport

The Hartsfield-Jackson Airport aviation firefighters raced to the plane in a fire truck.

At major airports, air traffic controllers work in control towers. They help pilots move planes safely in the air and on the ground so that they do not crash with other aircraft. Air traffic controllers also direct aviation firefighters to fire emergencies.

One-Minute Reaction

The airport's aircraft rescue and fire fighting (ARFF) team got to the plane just one minute after the pilot's call for help. The firefighters sprayed the flames with white **foam** that shot out from a **turret** on their huge truck. Then they searched the smoky plane to see if anyone was trapped inside.

Aviation firefighters work with an airplane's crew to get passengers out of the plane safely during an emergency.

Aviation firefighters use a special truck, called an ARFF truck, to spray an airplane fire with foam.

In less than 15 minutes, the ARFF team had put out the fire and helped **evacuate** everyone. Five passengers, two crew members, and one firefighter were taken to a hospital for medical treatment. Luckily, because of the firefighters' quick action, nobody died in the fire.

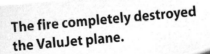

The fire completely destroyed the ValuJet plane.

Intense Fires

Airplane fires, such as the one in Atlanta, can break out during takeoff or landing, or after a crash. The **fuel** that is burned to power the plane's engines causes most of the fires. If there's a fuel leak, the highly **flammable** liquid may catch fire. Flames can then quickly spread throughout the aircraft.

The fire on ValuJet 597 started when pieces of metal from the engine broke off and smashed into the fuel line, or hose. Leaking fuel caught fire and the flames spread to the cabin.

Aviation firefighters wear special suits to protect themselves from deadly flames. Airplane fuel fires can get as hot as 2,500°F (1,371°C)!

Fortunately, aviation firefighters at airports across the world are trained to battle these deadly fires. For example, they know that water alone won't put out the blazes because flames from a fuel fire are much hotter than those from building fires. Instead, aviation firefighters spray foam—a mix of water, chemicals, and air—which puts out these extremely hot fires better than water.

Aviation firefighters spray foam from an ARFF truck (right) and from a hose (below).

Poisonous Smoke

Aviation firefighters know that during an airplane fire, the deadliest danger for passengers is smoke. Much of the plane's cabin, including the walls, is made of plastic. When it burns, the plastic gives off hot, poisonous **fumes**. If people breathe it in, they may die from the poisonous smoke or from the heat burning their lungs.

On a burning plane, passengers are more likely to die from breathing in smoke than from getting burned.

In August 1985, smoke **inhalation** led to **tragedy** on British Airtours Flight 28M. As the plane sped down a runway in England, an engine fire broke out. Black smoke quickly filled the cabin. Many people could not escape in time because they couldn't see the emergency **exits**. Most of the 55 people who died in the fire were killed from breathing in smoke.

After the British Airtours tragedy, stronger safety rules were put into effect. For example, floor lights are now required on planes so passengers can find the emergency exits in dark, smoky cabins.

The fire on the British Airtours plane started in the left engine just before the aircraft took off. Firefighters were able to rescue 136 people from the plane.

Evacuate!

People on a burning plane can die in just minutes from breathing in smoke, so aviation firefighters have to be lightning quick. If flames are blocking the emergency exits, firefighters first spray foam on the doors. This creates a fire-free path that allows people to evacuate.

Some people who are rescued may be suffering from smoke inhalation, burns, or other injuries. Firefighters provide **first aid** to injured people before they are taken to a hospital.

Once the blaze is under control, crew members open the emergency exit doors and set up **inflatable** slides so passengers can get down to the ground. Firefighters then search the plane for people who have passed out or are trapped in the cabin. They use special tools to pry open **cockpit** doors or bathroom doors that are stuck.

The engine of this Air India plane caught fire just before takeoff at an airport in Mumbai, India, in September 2009. Over 200 passengers used slides to evacuate the plane.

Firefighting Truck

The best weapon that aviation firefighters have to battle aircraft fires is the ARFF truck. Although this life-saving vehicle is extremely heavy—about 88,000 pounds (39,916 kg)—it can still reach a speed of 50 miles per hour (80.5 kph) in just 35 seconds. This allows firefighters to **respond** to a burning plane in a hurry.

joystick

The inside of an ARFF truck

Much of the equipment on an ARFF truck is operated by just one ARFF team member. He or she uses **joysticks** to aim and control the amount of foam that is sprayed from the turrets.

ARFF
380

LAX LOS ANGELES CITY FIRE DEPARTMENT

Once on the scene, firefighters use the ARFF truck's equipment to save as many lives as possible. For example, they use turrets to spray more than 3,000 gallons (11,356 l) of foam per minute. A sharp, pointed **nozzle** attached to an arm on top of the truck can punch a hole in an aircraft and spray foam inside the cabin. Firefighters also hold hoses attached to the truck and aim foam onto burning airplanes.

Cabin-piercing nozzle

Turret

Turret

Special Training

Only the best training can prepare someone to become an aviation firefighter. At special training schools, students study the designs of many types of airplanes. This helps them learn how to fight fires in any part of an aircraft, including the fuel tank and all the exits. Students learn the designs so well that they can draw diagrams of them by heart.

Airports, like this one in London, England, have many buildings, runways, and airplanes. During training, aviation firefighters learn how to reach any location at an airport quickly.

As part of their training, aviation firefighters also practice rescues in **mock** planes. Students climb ladders to get onto a plane while carrying heavy equipment. They are taught how to search every part of an aircraft where injured people might be trapped. During a real emergency, scared passengers may scream and push each other. Therefore, aviation firefighters also learn how to calm down hundreds of people and safely direct them through small emergency exits.

Many airports prefer that aviation firefighter students already have experience working as **urban** firefighters.

Eva Plessing finished her aviation firefighting training in 2013.

Aviation firefighter students practice rescuing people.

Behind the Scenes

Airplane fires don't happen often. So what do aviation firefighters do when they're not putting out fires? According to Stephen Kilby, chief of ARFF at Miami International Airport in Florida, firefighters spend most of their time maintaining their equipment and preparing for aircraft emergencies.

Aviation firefighting equipment stands ready at Los Angeles International Airport in California.

Every day, Chief Kilby's team of aviation firefighters tests the lights, sirens, nozzles, and turrets on the ARFF trucks. They also check the water and chemicals inside the trucks that are used to make foam. The team drives around the airport to make sure every area is safe. The firefighters review their first-aid skills as well. This helps them stay ready. According to Chief Kilby, "When an aircraft comes in the middle of the night with problems, you've got to put on your gear, get there, and try to save a life."

Aviation firefighters take turns working 24-hour **shifts**. During their long shifts, they cook and eat their meals at the airport, and they sleep there, too.

Practice, Practice, Practice

In May 2013, not one but two planes caught fire on the runway at Dulles Airport in Washington, D.C. When the airport's aviation firefighters arrived, they saw clouds of black smoke. They heard the terrified screams of injured passengers.

These aviation firefighters are spraying foam on a plane that was set on fire so they could practice putting out blazes.

This was not a disaster, however, and no one was in real danger. The airport was holding a practice **drill**. The fires were set on purpose, and the **victims** were actors. These emergency exercises give firefighters a chance to practice the firefighting and first-aid skills they learned in training. Even though very few aircraft fires and crashes actually occur, firefighters must always be prepared for a real disaster.

During a practice drill, actors wear makeup to look like injured victims of a plane crash. Dummies are used to look like people who have been killed.

 The Federal Aviation Administration (FAA) is a United States government agency that sets safety standards for airports. The FAA requires airports to hold practice drills every three years.

21

Many Jobs

At a busy airport, aviation firefighters race to help out during any life-threatening situation, not just fires. For example, they help people who are wounded in bus or car accidents near the airport. Inside an aircraft or **terminal**, they also provide first aid to people who become ill. The firefighters are always ready for action when they get the message, "We have a medical emergency!"

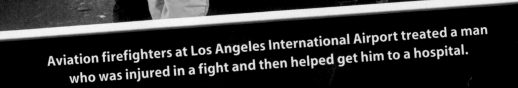

Aviation firefighters at Los Angeles International Airport treated a man who was injured in a fight and then helped get him to a hospital.

Aviation firefighters don't just rescue people, however. Sometimes animals, such as stray dogs, wander onto a runway. These animals are in danger of being run over by planes. In addition, if a pilot tries to veer away from an animal, the plane may crash. To prevent this from happening, aviation firefighters are often responsible for catching these animals.

Sometimes, people travel with **venomous** animals, such as snakes or scorpions. If they get loose in a terminal, the animals may bite or sting people. Aviation firefighters provide medical care to people who have been injured by animals.

Scorpions (left) and a cobra (above)

Tragedy in Spain

Despite their amazing skills, aviation firefighters cannot always save everyone in an emergency. In August 2008, Spanair Flight 5022 crashed just after it left the ground in Madrid, Spain. The plane went down in a wooded area near the runway and **exploded** into a fireball. Flames quickly spread to the trees surrounding the airport.

Parts of the plane broke apart when it crashed.

Hundreds of emergency workers responded. ARFF trucks from the airport, fire engines from a local fire department, and **ambulances** sped to the crash site. Firefighters were able to put out the raging fire in two hours. Rescue workers fought heroically to save the passengers and crew members. Sadly, though, 154 people died. Only 18 people survived the crash.

Helicopters helped firefighters on the ground by dropping water from large buckets onto the fire.

All the crew members aboard Spanair Flight 5022 died in the crash. Several passengers rescued by firefighters died from their injuries after they reached the hospital.

Science for Safety

In order to make aircraft fires less deadly, experts are finding better ways to help firefighters battle them. For example, scientists are developing slower-burning materials for airplane cabin walls, chairs, and carpets. These new materials slow down the spread of flames and poisonous smoke. As a result, firefighters will have more time to rescue people aboard a burning airplane.

Scientists are also developing a foam-spraying robot! Aviation firefighters can use a remote control to guide the robot near the most dangerous aircraft fires without risking their lives.

The newest **technology** can help make air travel safer. However, life-threatening emergencies can still occur. When that happens, highly trained aviation firefighters are always ready to risk their own lives to save others.

Aviation firefighters do whatever it takes to save people from deadly airplane fires.

Aviation Firefighters' Gear

Aviation firefighters wear special clothing as they fight aircraft fires. Here is some of their gear.

The *coat* and *pants* have an aluminum coating that protects a firefighter from heat and flames.

Thick, heavy *boots* protect an aviation firefighter's feet.

Special *gloves* stand up to even the hottest flames from a fuel fire.

An ARFF *helmet* protects a firefighter's head, face, and eyes. It is made of heat-resistant and fire-resistant materials.

Aviation firefighters also use many tools to fight fires.

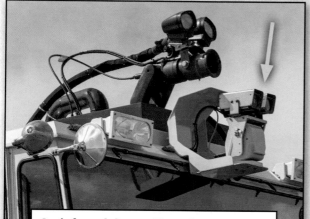

An *infrared thermal imaging camera* is attached to the roof of an ARFF truck. It can zoom in to find people who are trapped in dark, smoky cabins.

A *Jaws of Life* is strong enough to cut through metal or plastic doors on a plane.

A *Halligan* can pry open locked or stuck doors.

Sometimes, an aviation firefighter will wear a mask and an air tank called an SCBA (Self-Contained Breathing Apparatus), which provides clean, fresh air and lessens the risk of smoke inhalation.

Glossary

ambulances (AM-byuh-*lihnss*-iz) vehicles that carry sick or injured people to a hospital

aviation (*ay*-vee-AY-shuhn) the science of building and flying aircraft

cabin (KAB-in) the part of an airplane where the passengers sit

cockpit (KOK-pit) the front part of an airplane, where the pilot and co-pilot sit

crew (KROO) a group of people who work together to get a job done; on an airplane, the crew includes the pilot, co-pilot, and several flight attendants

drill (DRIL) an exercise or activity that is practiced over and over

evacuate (i-VAK-yoo-ayt) to remove from a dangerous area

exits (EG-zits) escape routes

exploded (ek-SPLOH-did) blew apart with a loud bang and great force

first aid (FURST AYD) care given to an injured or sick person in an emergency before he or she is treated by a doctor

flammable (FLAM-uh-buhl) able to easily catch fire

foam (FOHM) lots of very small bubbles made when liquid and air mix together

fuel (FYOO-uhl) something that is burned to produce heat or energy, such as wood, coal, or gasoline

fumes (FYOOMZ) harmful gas or smoke given off by chemicals or something that is burning

inflatable (in-FLAY-tuh-buhl) able to be blown up with air, like a balloon

inhalation (*in*-huh-LAY-shuhn) the act of breathing in

joysticks (JOI-stiks) devices used to control movement in a vehicle or aircraft

mock (MOK) not real

nozzle (NAHZ-uhl) a spout at the end of a hose or tube that shoots out liquid

respond (ri-SPOND) to arrive at the scene of an emergency to provide help

runway (RUHN-*way*) a special road used by airplanes for taking off and landing

shifts (SHIFTS) set periods of time in which people work

technology (tek-NOL-uh-jee) the science of making useful things

terminal (TUR-muh-nuhl) a building at an airport where passengers arrive and depart on airplanes

tragedy (TRAJ-uh-dee) a terrible event that causes great sadness or suffering

turret (TUHR-it) a part on the top or front of a truck that turns and shoots foam or water in different directions

urban (UR-buhn) having to do with cities

venomous (VEN-uhm-uhss) able to attack with a poisonous bite

victims (VIK-tuhmz) people who have been hurt or killed

Bibliography

Anderson, Jim, Jeff Hawkins, and Robert Gill. *Aircraft Accidents: A Practical Guide for Responders.* Clifton Park, NY: Thomson Delmar Learning (2008).

IFSTA (International Fire Service Training Association). *Aircraft Rescue and Fire Fighting.* Stillwater, OK: Fire Protection Publications, Oklahoma State University (2008).

Shapiro, Larry. *Fighting Fire: Trucks, Tools, and Tactics.* Minneapolis, MN: MBI (2008).

Read More

Barber, Nicola. *Plane Crash (Emergency!).* Mankato, MN: Arcturus (2012).

Goldish, Meish. *Firefighters to the Rescue (The Work of Heroes: First Responders in Action).* New York: Bearport (2012).

Spalding, Frank. *Plane Crash: True Stories of Survival (Survivor Stories).* New York: Rosen (2007).

Learn More Online

To learn more about aviation firefighters, visit
www.bearportpublishing.com/FireFight

Index

aircraft rescue and firefighting (ARFF) 6–7, 9, 14–15, 18–19, 25, 28–29

air traffic controllers 5

animals 23

Atlanta, Georgia 4, 8

British Airtours Flight 28M 11

control tower 5

crash 5, 8, 21, 23, 24–25

crew 4, 6–7, 13, 25

drills 21

Dulles Airport 20

England 11, 16

equipment 5, 6, 14–15, 17, 18, 28–29

evacuation 7, 12–13

explosion 24

Federal Aviation Administration (FAA) 21

first aid 13, 19, 21, 22

foam 6, 9, 12, 14–15, 19, 26

fuel 8–9, 16, 28

gear 19, 28–29

Hartsfield-Jackson International Airport 4–5

hoses 8–9, 15

joysticks 14

Kilby, Chief Stephen 18–19

Los Angeles International Airport 18, 22

Madrid, Spain 24

Miami International Airport 18, 23

Mumbai, India 13

nozzles 15, 19

passengers 4, 6–7, 10–11, 12–13, 17, 20, 25

pilot 5, 6, 23

plastic 10, 29

Plessing, Eva 17

radio 5

robot 26

runway 5, 11, 16, 20, 23, 24

slides 13

smoke 4, 6, 10–11, 12, 20, 26, 29

smoke inhalation 11, 12, 29

Spanair Flight 5022 24–25

training 9, 16–17, 21, 27

trucks 5, 6, 9, 14–15, 19, 25, 29

turrets 6, 14–15, 19

ValuJet Flight 597 4–5, 6–7, 8

Washington, D.C. 20

About the Author

Nancy White has written many nonfiction books for children. She lives just north of New York City, in the Hudson River Valley.